Visit Egypt!

Jill Laidlaw

Published 2009 by
A & C Black Publishers Ltd.
36 Soho Square, London, W1D 3QY
www.acblack.com

ISBN HB 978-1-4081-0862-8
         PB 978-1-4081-1285-4

Series consultant: Gill Matthews

This book is produced using paper that is made from wood grown in managed, sustainable forests. It is natural, renewable and recyclable. The logging and manufacturing processes conform to the environmental regulations of the country of origin.

Produced for A & C Black by Calcium.
Printed and bound in China by C&C Offset Printing Co.

All the internet addresses given in this book were correct at the time of going to press. The author and publishers regret any inconvenience caused if addresses have changed or sites have ceased to exist, but can accept no responsibility for any such changes.

Acknowledgements
The publishers would like to thank the following for their kind permission to reproduce their photographs:
Cover: Shutterstock; Istockphoto: Ben McLeish. **Pages:** Corbis: The Art Archive 14, The Gallery Collection 11, Mike Nelson/epa 13, Roger Wood 15; Dreamstime: Mahmoudmahdy 7; Fotolia: Cambo 16; Istockphoto: Karim Hesham 6; Rex Features: Quilici / Iverson 12; Shutterstock: Vaju Ariel 21, WH Chow 5, Mirek Hejnicki 19, André Klaassen 20, Michal Kram 9, Mary Lane 8, Bill McKelvie 17, Marco_tb 10, Styve Reineck 18. **Map:** Geoff Ward 4.

Contents

Land of Sun

Welcome to the Arab Republic of Egypt in northern Africa. What do you think you will see here? Egypt is a country of contrasts. You can find deserts next to rich farmland and ancient pyramids can be seen from modern skyscraper hotels.

Mediterranean Sea

Alexandria

Cairo

Giza

Lower Egypt

River Nile

Karnak

Valley of the Queens

Luxor

Red Sea

Valley of the Kings

Upper Egypt

Aswan

Abu Simbel

This map of Egypt shows some of the main sites to visit.

Getting here

The easiest and quickest way to get to Egypt is by plane. The cities of Cairo, Luxor, and Aswan all have modern airports. Once you are here you can travel from city to city by air, rail, or road. We also have camels, hot-air balloons, horse-drawn taxis, and sail boats.

Year-round sun

Egypt is the perfect holiday destination for anyone who enjoys the heat. We have two seasons – winter and summer. Winter is from October/November to March. The temperature stays between 11°C (52°F) and 18°C (64°F). Summer is from April to October. From June to July the average temperature is 29°C (84°F), but it can rise to 50°C (122°F)!

The Nile Valley

Come to the Nile Valley. This is where the ancient Egyptians built many pyramids and temples.

You can see:
- the Great Pyramid at Giza
- temples at Luxor and Karnak
- the Valley of the Kings
- the Valley of the Queens
- mortuary temples of the dead
- the temples of Abu Simbel

The River Nile is the main highway of Egypt. It is also the world's longest river. Take a journey along the Nile in a cruise ship. You will see over 5,000 years of history in a week.

 Travel Tip

The tourist season in Egypt is during the winter, from October to March. The cooler air makes it more comfortable for sightseeing.

Traditional boats, called *feluccas*, on the River Nile.

The Biggest Pyramid on Earth

Catch a ride to Giza, at the edge of Cairo, to see the pyramids here. You must visit the Great Pyramid. It is the biggest pyramid in Egypt. It was built for Pharaoh Khufu who ruled from around 2551 to 2528 BC. Step back in time 4,500 years as soon as you get off the bus.

The Great Pyramid is made of over 2 million blocks of limestone.

Dark tunnels

I hope you are not afraid of small spaces. The entrance to the Great Pyramid is a narrow, low corridor. It is very dark, hot, and cramped. The corridor plunges down into the pyramid, leading to an unfinished chamber. Next, move into a small tunnel and climb upwards. This will take you to the Queen's Chamber.

Did you know?

The base alone of the Great Pyramid is as large as eight football pitches.

Grave robbers

From the Queen's Chamber, climb higher into the Grand Gallery. It is a huge space – it is 47 m (154 ft) long and the roof hovers 8 m (26 ft) above your head.

Now climb beyond the Gallery to the King's Chamber. This is the heart of the pyramid. Here you will see Khufu's **sarcophagus**. Grave robbers stole everything else centuries ago. The sarcophagus, made of red stone called granite, was too heavy to lift so the robbers had to leave it!

Travel Tip

Drink lots of water – if you don't you may get ill because of the heat.

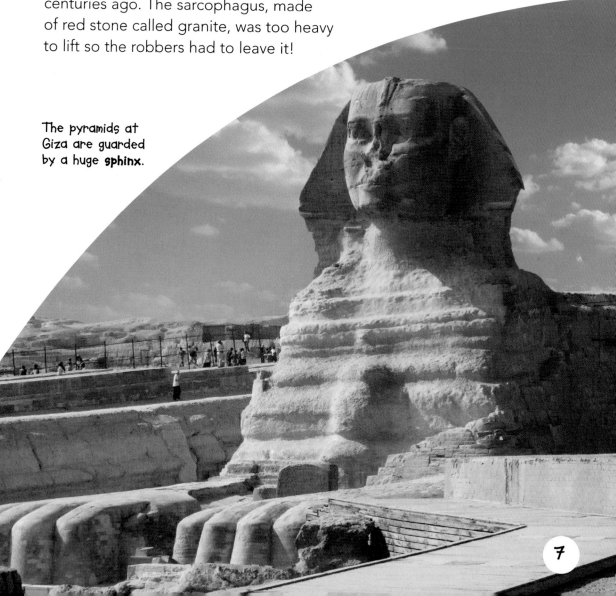

The pyramids at Giza are guarded by a huge **sphinx**.

Temples of the Gods

Once you have seen the Great Pyramid, take a boat down the River Nile to see two of our finest temple sites.

Luxor Temple

The modern town of Luxor was built on top of Thebes, which was the capital of Egypt around 1991 BC. The Temple of Luxor sits near the waterfront, on the east bank of the river.

The columns inside Luxor Temple are decorated with beautiful paintings.

Past times

- King Amemhotep III reigned from about 1402 to 1364 BC. He started Luxor Temple and dedicated it to the gods **Amun-Ra**, **Mut**, and **Khonsu**.

- The ancient Egyptians left Thebes and it became covered by the sand of the desert. It was buried and forgotten for thousands of years.

- Luxor Temple was rediscovered in 1885. The buildings that surrounded it were cleared away to reveal the ancient temple.

 Travel Tip

There's a light and sound show at Karnak. It displays all Karnak's magnificent history in a fun way, three times a night in the tourist season.

Karnak

The largest surviving ancient religious site in the world is at Karnak. It is near Luxor.

A limestone statue at the Temple of Amun at Karnak.

The Precinct of Amun

The temple complex at Karnak has different parts, called precincts. These contain many temples – there's enough room here for ten cathedrals.

Some of the things you can see in the Precinct of Amun.

- A walkway of splendid sphinxes with the bodies of lions and the heads of rams.

- "Pylons" or temple gateways. The first pylon you come to is 43 m (141 ft) high – it is the tallest one in Egypt.

- The Temple of **Rameses II**, one of the most famous pharaohs of ancient Egypt.

- Two massive statues, called colossi, of Rameses II.

- The Great Hypostyle Hall – a hall of 140 huge stone pillars.

The Valley of the Kings

The Valley of the Kings is the pharaohs' graveyard. It takes up an entire valley. The pyramids kept being robbed, so they began to bury the pharaohs in the Valley of the Kings in tombs cut deep into the rock. But the tombs were also robbed.

How to get there

The Valley of the Kings is opposite Luxor, on the west bank of the River Nile. You can catch a ferry across the river and then take a taxi or hire a bicycle.

Which valley?

The area is split into two – the east valley and the west valley. Most tourists visit the east valley – there are lots of tombs to see, including that of Tutankhamun. The west valley only has one tomb open to the public.

TUT

🧳 Travel Tip

You must buy tickets to go into the tombs. You need to buy a separate ticket for the tomb of Tutankhamun.

The entrance to Tutankhamun's tomb.

Tomb entry

How many tombs do you think you could see in one day? Probably only about three or four. Not all of the tombs are open – some are closed for study and some are kept closed to protect them.

This is a painting of Pharaoh Rameses II. His tomb is found in the Valley of the Kings.

Top four to see

- The tomb of Rameses IV – it has been a tourist attraction for thousands of years.

- The tomb of Tutankhamun. This is the most famous tomb in the Valley. See pages 12–13.

- The tomb of the sons of Rameses II. It is thought to have about 120 rooms!

- The tomb of **Tuthmosis III**, one of the oldest in the Valley.

Tutankhamun

Right in the heart of the Valley of the Kings is the tomb of Tutankhamun, the most famous pharaoh in the world. He was crowned ruler of Egypt when he was only nine years old, but he died at the age of 19 or 20.

Tutankhamun's tomb is very small. This is because he wasn't a very important pharaoh. His tomb was discovered in 1922 with most of its treasures still safe inside.

Tutankhamun's body was discovered inside a huge stone sarcophagus.

Was the king murdered?

Tutankhamun died very suddenly and was buried in a hurry – look at the pictures on the walls of the tomb. Paint has been splashed on some of them as if they were finished in a rush. No one knows how Tutankhamun died. Some people think he was murdered. Some people think he broke his leg, perhaps in a chariot accident, and died afterwards from the infected wound.

Treasures

Some of the things found in Tutankhamun's tomb were:

- Eight baskets of 3,000-year-old fruit.

- A solid gold mask, which was placed on his face after his death (see page 21).

Gaze upon the face of Tutankhamun inside his burial chamber.

The face of a pharaoh

You can see Tutankhamun for yourself when you go into his burial chamber. Remember to be quiet to show your respect for the person who is buried here. Tutankhamun's body is wrapped in linen and is on display in a glass box. You can even see his face. The temperature inside the box is controlled by a computer, to stop the mummy from decaying.

🧳 Travel Tip

Go to the Egyptian Museum in Cairo to see the things that were in Tutankhamun's tomb (see pages 20–21).

The Valley of the Queens

It's not just pharaohs who are buried in the Valley of the Kings – nobles, royal wives, and royal children are buried there, too.

Around 1300 BC work started on the Valley of the Queens, near the Valley of the Kings. This was to be a separate place for wives to be buried. But some wives were still buried with their husbands in the Valley of the Kings.

Despite being thousands of years old, this wall painting from **Nefertari's** tomb is still very bright.

Less space

Many of the tombs in the Valley of the Queens are built to the same basic plan as the tombs in the Valley of the Kings – they are just smaller. They have an entrance, a corridor, a few rooms, and finally a burial chamber.

Did you know?

There are over 80 tombs in the Valley of the Queens, but most of them are closed to the public. You can only visit four tombs.

Nefertari

The most famous tomb in the Valley of the Queens belongs to Nefertari, the favourite wife of pharaoh Rameses II. Nefertari's tomb is the biggest in the valley. The wall paintings in this tomb are beautiful, but very fragile.

Paintings of Nefertari decorate the walls of her tomb.

Be warned!

- Only 150 people are allowed to visit Nefertari's tomb each day – so turn up early.

- You'll have to wear a mask because your breath can damage the paintings.

- You'll have to wear shoe covers to stop dust coming into the tomb and causing more harm.

💼 Travel Tip

You are not allowed to take photographs in the tombs. Flash photography can harm the paintings. You leave your camera at the door.

Temples of the Dead

The ancient Egyptians didn't just build temples to the gods – they also built temples to worship dead pharaohs. These temples are called mortuary temples. There are lots of mortuary temples near the Valley of the Kings. Most of them are in ruins.

Hatshepsut's temple

The most beautiful temple of all belongs to Hatshepsut, the wife of **Tuthmosis II**. When her husband died, Hatshepsut decided to rule Egypt instead of her nephew, the next in line to the throne. She ruled from 1490 to 1468 BC. You can visit the three floors of Hatshepsut's temple – the two bottom ones would have been filled with hundreds of trees and perfumed fountains.

Smashed to pieces

When Hatshepsut's nephew, Tuthmosis III, finally came to the throne he gave orders for all the buildings Hatshepsut created to be destroyed – including her temple. **Egyptologists** have been slowly putting the temple back together again – sometimes rebuilding a statue or a wall from thousands of pieces of stone.

The terraces of Queen Hatshepsut's temple can still be clearly seen today.

The ghost village

Behind the mortuary temples there's a walled village, called Deir al Madina. The village is now empty but once it was home to the best craftsmen in Egypt. They worked on the surrounding tombs and temples. The craftsmen were kept away from other people so that they couldn't tell anyone where the pharaohs' tombs could be found.

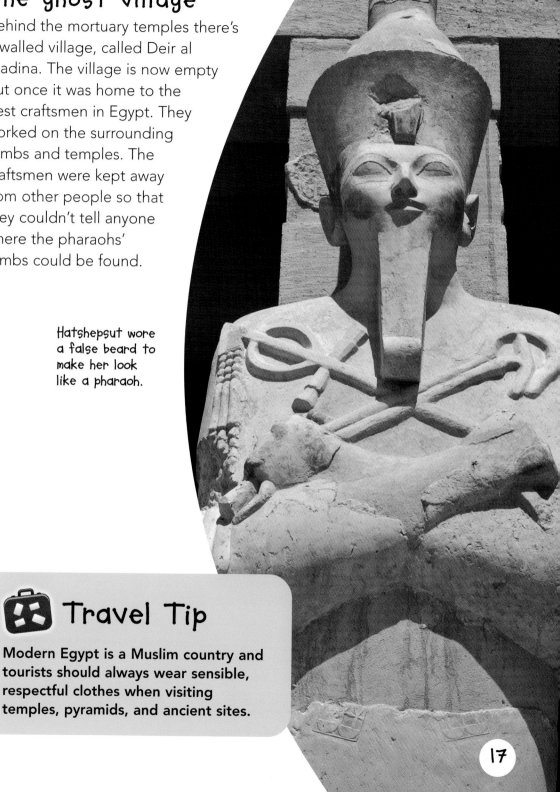

Hatshepsut wore a false beard to make her look like a pharaoh.

🧳 Travel Tip

Modern Egypt is a Muslim country and tourists should always wear sensible, respectful clothes when visiting temples, pyramids, and ancient sites.

The World's Biggest Jigsaw

In 1964, the Egyptian government decided to build a dam across the River Nile at a place called Aswan. But building the dam would flood the temples at nearby Abu Simbel. The temples were cut into 1,036 pieces. Then they were moved 60 m (196 ft) higher up the cliff so they were safe from the water. They were then put back together again like a giant, heavy jigsaw puzzle.

Getting there

The best way to get to Abu Simbel is by boat – river trips leave Cairo for Aswan every week.

Temples of Rameses II

Around 1257 BC the great Pharaoh Rameses II ordered his workmen to cut two temples out of the rock on the west bank of the Nile, just south of Aswan. One of the temples was for Rameses and the other was for his favourite wife, Nefertari.

The walls of Abu Simbel are carved with images of Ancient Egypt.

The main hall

The biggest chamber is called the Hypostyle Hall. It has eight 10 m (32 ft) high statues of Rameses dressed as the god Osiris, ruler of the dead.

As you move into the cliff, the rooms become smaller and smaller until you reach the "sanctuary". This is a room that contains the statues of Rameses and Amun-Ra, **Ra-Horakhte**, and **Ptah**, the gods the temple is dedicated to.

Travel Tip

When visiting Aswan try some of the local food. Vine leaves stuffed with spiced meat, roast pigeon, and kebabs are all very popular.

Four statues of Rameses sit outside the entrance to his temple.

A Place of Wonders

When you are in Cairo you must visit the Egyptian Museum in Tahrir Square – it has the most wonderful collection of ancient Egyptian objects in the world. About 7,000 people visit the museum every day.

What's inside?

There are nearly 90 rooms in the Egyptian Museum, spread over two floors. You can see:

- coins
- sculptures
- coffins
- jewellery
- chariots
- musical instruments
- children's games
- boats
- mummies
- weapons

The oldest objects are on the ground floor – walking around is like taking a walk through ancient Egypt itself.

The Egyptian Museum in Cairo is lit up at night.

About 3,500 objects from Tutankhamun's tomb are on display in the museum, including his death mask (shown above).

Amazing articles

In the museum you will find:

- The mummies of 11 pharaohs

- The mummy of Rameses II. This pharaoh's body is very well preserved – he still has skin, teeth, and hair

- The solid gold mask of Tutankhamun

Every month the museum staff choose one special object to put on display.

Be quiet!

When you go into the room that has the mummies of pharaohs in it you will be asked to keep quiet out of respect for the dead people in the room.

 Travel Tip

Take lots of water – the museum is not air-conditioned and can get very hot!

Did you know?

The Egyptian Museum has so many objects that if you spent one minute looking at every single one of them, it would take nine months to see them all.

Glossary

Amun-Ra Amun-Ra was half the god of Thebes (the ancient capital of Egypt) and half sun god. He was shown as having the body of a man and the head of a ram

Egyptologists the name given to people who study ancient Egyptian history at any point between the fifth century BC and the fourth century AD

Khonsu the moon god, a god of the sky. He is shown as a human with a falcon head, wearing a large circle, like the moon

Mut wife of Amun-Ra. Mut was the mother goddess and the queen of all living things. She is often shown as a woman wearing a vulture headdress

Nefertari (c. 1300–1250 BC) the "Royal" or "Chief" queen of Pharaoh Rameses II. Nefertari married Rameses when she was 13 and he was 15

Ptah the god of architects and artists. Ptah created the plan for the universe. He looked like a man wrapped in white cloth and carried a long staff (stick)

Ra-Horakhte he was half the sun god Ra and half the falcon god Horus, who was god of the sky

Rameses II (c.1289–1224 BC) One of the most famous pharaohs of ancient Egypt. Rameses built lots of monuments, such as the two temples at Abu Simbel

sarcophagus the outer coffin left above ground. In ancient Egypt there could be several coffins inside the sarcophagus, so it could be very large

sphinx stone statue of a lion with the head of a man or woman

Tuthmosis II came to the throne of Egypt after the death of his father, Tuthmosis I. He was a weak pharaoh

Tuthmosis III (c.1490–1436 BC) the son of Tuthmosis II and the nephew of Hatshepsut. As pharaoh, Tuthmosis III became a great warrior king

Further Information

Websites

The website of the Egyptian Tourism office is full of information about the opening times of museums and pyramids, River Nile cruises, hotels, and tours. Visit it at:
www.egypt.travel

The British Museum website has information about ordinary people, pharaohs, pyramids, trade, writing, and the gods of ancient Egypt:
www.ancientegypt.co.uk

Join in the search for a missing archaeologist in Egypt in 1929! Click on Death in Sakkara at:
www.bbc.co.uk/history/ancient/egyptians

This Discovery website has a Build a Pyramid game:
www.discovery.com/games/pyramid/pyramid.html

Books

Ancient Egypt by Ting Morris. Franklin Watts (2007).

Look Around an Egyptian Tomb. Franklin Watts (2007).

Ancient Egypt by Jane Shutter. Wayland (2008).

Index